the must-have guidebook for

writing
publishing
presenting

featuring 150 pro tips
for career success

Monisha Arya, MD, MPH and Natalia Rodriguez, MPH

To our parents for always believing in us.

To our mentors for selflessly sharing their time to teach, support our growth, and cheer us on as we navigate our own paths.

Contents

How This Guidebook Will Help You with Career Success

Let this book be your virtual mentor. What you will find on the pages aren't rules; they are tips (well, some may be rules). They are tips based on decades of our own "wins." Now, we want you to win!

Here is your first pro tip: The number one factor that will determine your success is time. Time investing in you. Protecting time on your calendar every week is crucial. You can call it [your name] winning time.

There will be thrilling ups and disappointing downs...remember that rejection is simply "redirection."

Enjoy the journey.

Crushing Your Conference Experience

Tips for Designing a Winning Poster

No one wants to read paragraphs of content. Use bullets to highlight key points.

Don't make people squint. Stick to black font and at least 36 font size.

Consider alternatives to words. Use graphics, diagrams, or photos to increase visual appeal.

Help your reader follow the flow of the story. Use subheadings.

Don't bombard your audience with content. Include 30% white space.

Don't overwhelm your audience with colors. Use no more than 3 colors.

Let your audience connect with you. Embed your contact and social media info into a QR code.

Notes

Tips for Writing a Compelling Poster Script

Prepare for your presentation.
Like an actor, you will be performing in front of your poster.

Write a succinct script (<450 words).
Your presentation is to stimulate curiosity and dialogue.

Welcome your visitor.
State your name and institution name and thank your visitor for coming to your poster.

Hook your audience.
Start with an engaging fact or question to reel your audience into your presentation.

Tell a story.
Convince your visitor why the research was needed and share 3 results that help solve the problem.

Incorporate action cues in your script.
Plan actions such as [point to poster] and [dramatic pause].

Memorize your script.
Like an actor, you should rehearse your lines and actions in front of your poster.

Notes

Tips for Promoting Your Poster Presentation

Share on social media. Create posts to let your network know where and when you will be presenting.

Notify your institution's office of communications. Draft a press release that can be shared in your institution's newsletters.

Submit to your alumni newsletter. Write a blurb that can be shared with your alumni network.

Report to your professional organization. Share updates of your work to help advance your field.

Pitch to your local newspaper. Write a 100-word summary of how your work impacts your community.

Talk at the dinner table. Let your family and friends know about your work and its importance.

Include in your CV/resume. Inform future academic programs and employers of your accomplishment.

Notes

Tips for Winning Your Poster Presentation

Greet your visitors. Introduce yourself with your full name and the name of your institution.

Do not read off your poster. Draft a script and practice a smooth delivery.

Interact with your visitors. Ask open-ended questions to create dialogue.

Engage with your poster. Point to any figures when it is easier to show rather than tell.

Help your visitors understand the relevance of your research. Relate your work to everyday life.

Welcome feedback. Always ask if there are comments or questions.

Appreciate your visitor. Shake hands and thank your visitor by name.

Notes

Tips for Designing a Powerful Business Card

Provide key information.
Ensure your name, title, email, phone number, and website are included.

Prioritize visibility and readability.
Avoid thin, light, decorative, and script fonts in the main text.

Attract attention with color.
Add a pop of color to accent text and customize your card design.

Invest in quality.
Use at least 14-point cardstock and consider a textured or glossy finish.

Include a QR code.
Use a QR code to help others efficiently link to you or your work.

Promote your social media.
Add your handles to encourage others to engage in your online professional network.

Don't crowd the layout.
Use both sides of the card for your content.

Notes

Tips for Arriving Prepared to Shine at a Conference

Pack your business cards. Make it easy for your new connections to find you again.

Print copies of your CV or resume. Be prepared to pursue new opportunities if you meet the right person.

Study the conference program. Plan your time by selecting the sessions, talks, and events you want to attend.

Update your social media profiles. Be ready to meet and connect with others on a professional level.

Prepare to explore the conference locale. Pack comfortable clothes and perhaps a bathing suit, hiking shoes, or skis.

Dress to impress. Make sure to pack professional clothes, including dressy but comfortable shoes and a blazer.

Rest before you go. Get ready for days of excitement and exhaustion by starting out energized and well-rested.

Notes

Tips for Productive Networking at a Conference

Perfect your pitch.
Introductions are important; define who you are and what you do in 30 seconds.

Network beyond the conference space.
Invite people you meet for a conversation over a meal or a walk.

Use business cards to foster connections.
Give the people you meet a way to follow up with you.

Pay attention to social media.
Not all networking happens face-to-face.

Build your community.
Meet people of all stages of their careers to help widen your perspective.

Promote yourself.
Include your social media handles in presentations and posters.

Take notes of who you meet.
Within a week, follow-up with an email or personalized LinkedIn connection request.

Notes

Tips for a Worthwhile and Enjoyable Conference Experience

It's not all work. Don't pass up social and networking opportunities while in the conference atmosphere.

Use social media. Use the conference hashtag to meet other attendees and stay up to date on conference activities.

Speak up, provide input, and ask questions. You are there to learn and network.

Take breaks. Conference days are long; recharge with coffee, a walk, or even a nap.

Diversify your learning. Attend talks and presentations that are outside the scope of your field.

Don't be overwhelmed. You can't do everything and meet everyone; enjoy what you can.

Leave the conference space. Make time to explore a new city on your own or with new connections.

Notes

Crushing Writing and Publishing

Tips for Writing an Engaging Manuscript Introduction

What is the problem?
Write 1-2 sentences introducing the problem you hope to solve.

Why is the problem important?
Write 2-3 sentences that give context to the problem to justify the study.

Why is there a problem?
Among the many reasons, focus on the 1-2 that your study addressed.

What is your solution?
In 1-2 sentences, explain your idea for solving the problem.

Explicitly state your study objective in one sentence.
"The objective of this study was…"

Don't include the details of how you tested your solution.
Save the 'how' for the Methods section.

Don't be wordy.
If you have a sentence that is over 3 lines of text, break it up or shorten it.

Notes

Tips for Key Elements of a Manuscript Methods Section

Recognize that location matters.
Include the city, state, and setting of the study.

Define the participants.
List the inclusion and exclusion criteria.

Supply the right details at the right time.
Save the number of participants for the Results section.

Share the participant requirements.
Describe the tasks that participants were asked to complete.

Allow others to follow in your footsteps.
Describe how the research staff gathered the data.

Mind the tense.
Use past tense when describing the procedures of your study.

Acknowledge institutional support.
Most journals require a statement of IRB approval.

Notes

Tips for a Neatly Structured Manuscript Results

Gather your reader's focus.
Remind them of your study objective in the first sentence.

Chunk your information.
Use subheadings to streamline and clarify results.

Show don't tell.
Design tables and figures to display results in an alternate format.

Stay organized.
Consider your research question and methods, and follow a chronological order.

Numbering order matters.
Number figures and tables according to how they are mentioned in the text.

Follow convention.
Start with total number of participants, move to subgroup demographics, then reveal study results.

Prepare for the discussion section.
Summarize key findings in a clear and concise concluding sentence.

Notes

Tips for a Striking Manuscript Discussion Section

Connect the dots. Summarize the results addressing your study objective.

Acknowledge unexpected findings. These results may help guide future research or improve intervention implementation.

Give your results meaning. Opine on what your results imply.

Compare and contrast. Tell us how your results compare to what is currently known in the field.

Recognize limitations. Describe reasons why your study design could lead to incorrect interpretations.

Foreshadow. In 1-2 sentences, suggest what research should be done next.

End with a bang. Summarize why your research was helpful to advancing the field.

Notes

Tips for Including Helpful Tables & Figures in Your Manuscript

Refer to your tables and figures in the text. Use "See Table 1" to alert readers to look at the complementary results.

Be organized. Number tables and figures in the order in which they are cited in the text.

Avoid confusion. Spell out abbreviations even if they are already defined in the text.

Tables and figures should stand-alone. Readers may look only at your tables and figures to learn your study results.

Tables and figures need titles. At the top of each, include a brief, declarative title that summarizes the content.

Consider patterns, shading, and color. Some journals allow these to help draw attention to elements in your tables and figures.

Don't go overboard. Journals have limits on the number of tables and figures.

Notes

Tips for Using Team-Writing to Complete a Manuscript in 6 Weeks

Team size matters. 3-4 writers is effective, efficient, and manageable.

Share ownership. Assign each team member a manuscript section to draft.

Recognize team member strengths. Someone with artistic talent may be assigned figures and tables.

Meet weekly to review drafts. In-person meetings create trust, ensure accountability, and stimulate progress.

Merge manuscript sections for a master draft to show on a big screen. At weekly team meetings, review the flow and assess the needs.

Use the line numbering function in Microsoft Word. Group feedback can occur efficiently if a team member can announce a line number for an edit or clarification need.

Celebrate weekly progress. Pats on the back, snacks, and simple thank yous make teamwork rewarding.

Notes

Tips for Match-Making Your Manuscript with an Ideal Journal

Read the journal's mission statement. Ensure your work will help the journal and its readers advance the field.

Get lucky. Check journals for a "call for papers" on a topic; you could be the right topic at the right time.

Impact factor matters. Ask a mentor if your work matches the expectation of the journal's impact factor.

Check your budget. If the journal charges any fees, ensure you have sufficient funding.

Count your words. Confirm your manuscript is within the journal's word count limit.

Don't be a copycat. Search the journal's recent publications to ensure you are adding complementary and novel knowledge.

There is not "one" perfect journal. Know your top 3 journals so you can confidently submit to another if rejected.

Tips written in collaboration with Rachel Marren. MPH

Notes

Tips for Key Finds in the Instructions for Authors

Complement the journal's theme.
Read your journal's purpose, scope, and policies before submission.

Find the word limit.
Different manuscript types have different word limits.

Look for specific formatting rules.
Journals vary in their publication formats.

Don't be overwhelmed by the length of instructions.
Print and highlight line items that apply to your submission.

Double check all requirements.
Ask co-authors or team members for help before submission.

Fine-tooth comb the instructions.
Look for any fees you may be charged.

Set reasonable reminder deadlines.
Make note of the submission review and decision turnaround time.

Notes

27

Tips for a Knockout Manuscript Cover Letter

Personalization matters. In the salutation, address the journal editor by name (e.g., Dr. Jones).

Announce your intention. State the type of manuscript you have chosen to submit (e.g., Brief Report, Commentary).

Read the journal's mission statement. In one sentence, proudly highlight how your work addresses this mission.

Have a hook. Succinctly and with passion describe 1-2 study results that you think will advance the field or help others.

Adhere to the instructions. Follow the cover letter requirements in the Instructions for Authors.

Make a good first impression. Run a spelling and grammar check on your cover letter.

Mind your manners. Conclude your letter with a thank you to the journal editor and staff for considering your work.

Notes

Tips for What to Do After You Submit Your Manuscript

Celebrate!
This milestone deserves a glass of wine, a beer, an ice cream, or a spa day.

Thank your team.
Update collaborators or behind-the-scenes help on this milestone.

Log on weekly.
Track your manuscript's journey through the review process via the journal's online portal.

Create a spreadsheet.
Keeps details like journal-assigned manuscript ID #, dates and results of weekly portal login, and editor contact information.

Strategize.
Research other journals and their requirements so you are immediately ready to submit to a new journal if Plan A fails.

Follow up.
If 6 weeks without an update, send a professional email to the editor kindly asking for a status update.

Check in with your team.
At week 8, share the manuscript's status and rereview the publishing game plan.

Notes

Tips for Successfully Communicating with a Journal Editor

Personalization matters.
In the salutation, address the journal editor by name (e.g., Dr. Jones).

Jog a memory.
Include the full title, journal-assigned, manuscript ID #, and date submitted.

Stay focused.
Be direct and to the point with your question or comment.

Be mindful of work-life balance.
Send your email during business hours.

Acknowledge the editor's manuscript review team.
Be thankful for their work behind the scenes.

Don't hide.
Provide multiple methods for the editor to contact you.

Show appreciation to the journal editor.
Thank them for their time, assistance, and effort.

Notes

Tips for Promoting Your Published Manuscript

Share on social media. Create a post with a key finding and a link to the full manuscript; repeat weekly with other findings.

Notify your communications office. Draft a 100-word summary of your work and highlight its relevance for a broader audience.

Submit to your alumni newsletter. Write a 100-word summary that can be shared with your alumni network.

Report to your professional organization. Share updates of your work to help advance your field.

Pitch to your local newspaper. Write a 250-word summary using "everyday language" to educate your community.

Share the news at the dinner table or on a work call. Let family, friends, and colleagues know about your work and its importance.

Include in your CV/resume. Inform future academic programs and employers of your accomplishment.

Notes

Tips for Handling Manuscript Rejection

Join the club.
Know that you are not alone; talk to peers or mentors for support.

Don't dwell.
Review your already-prepared list of journal options and quickly move on to Plan B.

Process your emotions...and then the reviewers' comments.
Reviewers aim to help you write a better piece.

Prepare for Plan B.
Review the Instructions for Authors for your Plan B journal.

Time is of the essence.
Within 7 days your manuscript should be in a new editor's hands.

Right place, right time.
You could be lucky the 2nd or 3rd or even 4th time submitting to other journals.

Stay determined.
Rejection is simply redirection.

Notes

Bonus Tips

Every opportunity is a learning experience. You will encounter successes and failures, but both will help you grow.

Self-promotion is not a bad word. Promoting your work will build your network and contribute to a greater good.

Pay it forward. Your experiences will bring to light tips that can help someone else's journey.

Notes

Acknowledgments

First, we would like to acknowledge and thank each other. We are a mentor-mentee powerhouse fortunate to have each other's support through individual and joint successes.

Thanks to Marie Flores-Korman, JD, of Tre H Publishing, for advising us as we neared the finish line.

Thanks to Kelly Schrank, MA, ELS, of Bookworm Editing Services, for sticking through the writing and planning process with us for two years.

Thanks to our financial mentor, Michele Cagan, CPA, for helping us establish MANR Communications for this book.

Thanks to Jenny Pan and to Lynsey Owens of Lynsey Creative for helping us formalize our book cover vision.

Thanks to Janhavi Govande for helping us learn about the process of book publishing.

Lastly, thanks to our family, friends, and colleagues for their unconditional support and generous feedback throughout our book writing journey.

Stay Connected!

Thank you for supporting 150 tips. We welcome your feedback and suggestions. We certainly want to hear about your wins!

Share on Twitter and please tag us @150Tips #150TipsBook.

Made in the USA
Middletown, DE
10 July 2022